"Hilary Jepsky is both a pictorial artist and a poet. And since her poems are beautiful and her pictures are too, the world is a more beautiful place because she is in it.

"This book is devoted to her poems. And while her poems are beautiful, many of them have an aspect that goes beyond mere beauty. They have an emotional content that reaches out and envelops the reader.

"Thus reading Hilary Jepsky is an experience that leaves you not quite the same again. Your appreciation of the world around you, and your sensitivity to it, are enhanced."

—Myron S. Kaufman

Remember Your Heart

Remember Your Heart

A Poetry Collection

Hilary Jepsky

iUniverse, Inc.
New York Lincoln Shanghai

Remember Your Heart

iUniverse books may be ordered through booksellers or by contacting:

iUniverse
2021 Pine Lake Road, Suite 100
Lincoln, NE 68512
www.iuniverse.com
1-800-Authors (1-800-288-4677)

ISBN: 978-0-595-42210-4 (pbk)
ISBN: 978-0-595-86550-5 (ebk)

Printed in the United States of America

For my grandmother Eva.

Contents

Acknowledgments

Thank you to Syed J. Rizvi for his invaluable editorial support.

Remember Your Heart

A Kiss

Brushes some love against my cheek.

By the river knees do bend. Mine.

I draw up the moon.

Close. Down to me.

I take a mouth to tenderly receive.

Love starved. Love graced. Poignant. Lost in the night.

Perhaps a dream I dared; a love song in the strands of my hair.

There is a token of a dream: of breast and thigh;

A caress from a lone branch as I rise.

The moon is my roundness; insistent of a last kiss.

I cannot rouse from night.

Alone. Waters from the river drift.

Yield to me water on skin.

Alabaster moon you are mine.

A Wedding Journey

Oh, husband, come to me on this day of wedding.

Fear not the years behind us.

Only think of the wholeness in this love.

I will make new memories for you from my heart and soul.

I shall wear the white of purity and bless it,

Not just on this day, but also, on the days to come.

Suffer not from the past. The future of wholeness is upon us.

In this understanding of compassion and completeness

Let us draw upon each other.

Holy is the birth of our journey of days.

The disappointment and sorrow of the past is gone.

Let us rejoice in the great joining of our good and kind natures.

Let us give to each other the sanctity of dreams.

Our days and nights complete each other.

I come to you all in white with purity of spirit,

All the days of our lives.

Ascension

Tender torsos harboring night;

Long drawn out rhythms of bodies in syncopation;

Primeval waters bathing limbs.

Lilies of a lake surrendering petals;

The hand that carves their very shape;

Defines the orbit circling the velvet ripples;

Waves of motion out to sea;

The moan of lips as one ascends.

The touch of her like a mermaid draws him in.

He becomes a sailor lured by her song.

They travel together on a bed born of sea.

The pivotal turns of desire are ridden,

Until the tides thrust them high to the shore.

Breathing to the surrender of lilies.

Each intricately carved petal is an offering of desire.

Lilt, the lilies as they ascend.

Beautiful Stranger

Oh, beautiful stranger, sweep me off my feet.

Take me to paradise: to heaven.

You and I will count stars like diamonds.

We will embrace, and embrace yet again.

Whisper that I am the angel you have dreamed of.

Take me with you to the green knoll by the river.

Let us lie among the daisies, and drink amber honey.

Oh, beautiful stranger, take me on a journey to a timeless land.

Gather me to your soul that I might have you all around me.

Oh, beautiful stranger, of mine, steal me away into the arms of night.

Oh, beautiful stranger, take me and yet take me again,

that I might hear your beating heart forever.

Believe

Herald the new day. I beckon you.

Hold the new song. I dare you.

Believe in the shining of the sky and hold fast.

Pray to the infinite horizon and leap far to it.

The shifting light of the hours plays upon you.

Beckon I at the ridge of the descending. Go ever deeper.

I wait there. I wait there for you.

You can love me because I descend ever deeper.

The time of the green ferns is approaching.

The land reclines far out to the far recesses.

The giving time is come to pass.

Adore the open meadow cradling the earth ever and after.

Go ever deeper.

We turn over earth and sky to shape the green.

Beneath My Skin

I shed my skin to see what lies beneath.

It is you.

It is you my love.

My heart beats beneath my skin for you, for you my love.

Your beautiful kiss: your one kiss impregnates me with love.

My ears hold your voice within: far within.

My hunger that arises is filled with completion by you.

When night finds my eyes I dream, I dream of you my love.

When the sun of morning opens my eyes,

I see you my love, beside me, close to me, my love.

You are my blessing. You are my sacred life.

You are beneath my skin.

It is you my love.

For My Child

Oh, my child, come to me.

Let me feel the beating of your small heart against mine.

Oh, let me touch you; your skin as fine as butterfly wings.

Come put your small hand in mine,

As we walk together in the meadow of buttercups.

The voices of birds are all around us.

Come my precious one;

Sit beside me that I might read you a story,

That only we two share.

Your laughter and impish charm are like that of an enchanted fairy.

Oh, my child let us glide together over a rainbow,

And find ourselves resplendent with color.

Fortune's Daughter

I carry my domain on my back.

All my close possessions are there: my sea shells,

My glass marbles, the golden key, a silver mirror and brush,

A kaleidoscope and a moonstone as big as a walnut.

I carry my life on my back as I travel near and far.

I am safe with my precious wonders.

Some want to barter and trade but I never do.

I believe the thing a person carries has a personal life of its own.

Carry your fortune and when at rest let those things spill forth.

I listen to my seashells.

I examine my precious marbles.

I hold that golden key.

My silver mirror and brush make me beautiful.

The kaleidoscope yields design and color and

My moonstone gathers moon beams in the night for me.

Golden Girl

You have waited for me; I am your golden girl.

I am the golden girl you keep in your pocket.

I am the golden girl among the green ferns.

I am the golden girl at the bottom of your coffee cup.

I am the golden girl at your garden gate; I am the golden girl at your gate.

Open.

I am the golden girl you fold around your heart.

I am the golden girl between your sheets.

I am the golden girl for I can do no wrong to you.

I am the golden girl who whispers from the moon to your ears.

I am the golden girl,

And I bless you as you sleep.

His Touch

He wore his love like a flame.

You could feel it burn deeply.

He knew how to get under a woman's skin.

Once he kissed you, your fate was sealed.

Once he took you there were no limits, no undisturbed spaces.

You knew without hesitation he charted a course.

He wore his love like a flame.

You could feel it burn deeply.

The depth like nothing you had felt.

What was his; what was yours was one.

He always knew what made your body tick.

He had only to enter your mouth,

Your hips and your body writhed with pleasure.

He wore his sex like a perfume; intoxicating; lingering long after.

Incantations

Late night time switches a frequency channelled deep into dreams.

I utter silent incantations.

Harbor me a charmed celestial orb within my bed.

The windowpanes draw close.

Ripe is the night dreamtime for the harvest of quilts.

Essential darkness spares all mystery to grow

Into the wood of the headboard.

The curtains rise and fall with wind breath.

Slumber lies upon earth.

Raises me the dreamer to balance night.

A persuasion to linger with a spectacle

Before dew drops hours away.

My incantations alight from dreamers' lips

To draw in all the song and sound that night can muster

From bed and board, orb and windowpane.

Let Me

Tell me your troubles.

I want to unburden you with a thought, a word, or a gesture.

Let me take away your tears, your pain, and your sorrow.

Trust me with your secret fears, your untold whisperings that surround you.

Let me in. Let me draw you close unto me.

Let me offer my breath unto you.

Let my arms embrace you like the solid trunk of a mighty tree.

I want to hold you.

I want to shelter and protect you from the worst that might befall you.

Let me in.

Draw upon my breath.

Let me in.

I will surround you with a deep peace.

I will never, ever let you fall.

Life

Hold on tight to life for life is precious.

Never deny yourself the pleasure of life.

Life is your joy and your completion.

Never give up on life

For then you will have nothing.

Each day say: "I live; I am alive;

I have been given life."

Life is your choice, your answer,

And your salvation.

Live. And yet live again.

Rise and walk with me into life.

Only give me your hand

and I will lead you into life.

I walk beside you for you are life itself.

I will take you into the beauty of day

And the tranquility of night.

I know your name well.

I name you again and again: life.

Life Embodied

Entwined is the circumference of life and death.

Seek like a contusion of choice; the way wound about chance.

Once a green leaf.

Now shrivelled brown.

Bounty of seasons.

The smallness of lost silence, shall the trees speak.

No the darkness overpowers.

Tall are the shadows that grasp.

The sun betrays the thirsty fruit.

The rain comes.

Takes the sun and fruit to the rivulet's down to a place timeless,

Where yet seedlings burst behind the trees erect,

Phallic root of life embodied.

Mary's Red Night

Mary swivels on her balcony;

The fiesta of her siesta.

Roses bloom in her hands.

She sways to the music surging within her breasts.

Butterflies alight. Twilight lingers. May birds sing.

The steady thrumming of spring blossoms play on the trees.

Silver flutes whisper her name.

The dancers begin. There is a yearning in their step.

The rose petals so full of velvet and red, cascade.

The serenade of Mary resounds.

Her balcony twinkles with a thousand evening stars.

Her brow is alive with butterflies and sound.

Her red dress emerges; a rose in the night sky.

A rose that takes flight.

Millenniums

The glacier melts.

The ices flow down to become pools of liquid.

My heart floats warm and serene.

The coaxing of your breath frees my body.

A primeval response buried for an eternity surfaces.

Layers of me within the frozen snows of myself recede.

Reflexes within my body thaw and respond to your pulse.

There is a joy replete in communion.

Your love dance thrusts far into me.

I unfurl from my center, like bees buzzing to the green places,

Where flowers wait to be received.

The heat of your desire comes like sun to shadow.

Hidden recesses long dead are reclaimed.

Life is hurdling the barriers of time; plunging towards new latitude.

A great gyration encompassing millenniums,

Rests within the proximity of sheer evolution,

Enfolding lush rainforests that bear ripe fruit.

Moon Dreams

The morning hour dawns.

Night-dreams pervade the air.

They linger upon our lips.

We call them close so as not to let the memory of them go.

We rise.

Our dreams follow us.

The moon of night diffuses the sun.

Are we back sleeping within our precious images?

The child with the golden hair and the laughing voice is so real.

The lapping of the bright blue water against the distant shore,

Shines complete with steady motion.

The emerald leaves of forest trees are drenched with morning dew.

Dreamers do not wake this morning so illumined by the

Round pearl of ivory moon.

Places

Mystify me.

Take me to places I've never been.

Seize the moment and move mountains.

Take me to that place high above.

I won't be daunted. Push me from a place that thrills me.

Let me stand among the beauty that exemplifies

Everything I want to behold.

Send me to the sound of rebounding laughter.

Throw me a line that extends forever.

Rouse me from my slumber to meet all my dreams.

Mystify me.

Bring magic that resounds in my ears.

Push me from a place that thrills me.

Release ten thousand butterflies to greet my eyes.

Take me to a velvet night to walk upon with love surrounding me.

Receive

Walk among giants. Walk with your head held high.

Your suffering is ended. Angels wait to hold you forever.

Walk on. Laugh with a light heart.

I have come for you:

I and no one else. Take my hand.

Together we will come to the high ground.

The grass is green and thick.

Be received. Walk among the immortal. Sing your song.

Stride among the vast humanity.

Sweep aside your foreboding.

Laughter and delight shall claim you.

See the morning glories wave before you.

Taste the sweetness of day and never forget who you are.

I am here. I and no one else.

Come and be received.

Redemption

The look in your eyes of a new lover, Redemption.

You were lost, now you are found.

Your lover inexorably takes every step with you in your mind.

You hold his image like a new red heart, worn invisibly upon your own.

Where his will beats; beats your own.

You relish his perfect kisses and the little pauses between each one.

Your pulse races as you go to meet him, Redemption.

It will not let you go, there is no future, and there is no past.

This is the moment you share, your lover waits for you now.

Sleep

I see out of the corner of my eye, your deep slumber,

Sleep, sleep, sleep within your vivid dreams.

Let your heart envelop you.

Let only gentle thoughts pervade your soul.

Let your mother's voice in song,

Arise from your childhood to fill you with her love.

I see out of the corner of my eye your breath rise and fall peacefully.

A slight smile forms upon your lips.

I bend and kiss your forehead for I am with you as you rest.

Your pillow cradles your head as I run my fingers through your hair.

Sleep gently; soothingly and soundly.

Sleep my angel.

Sleep.

Sleep.

Stars

From the replica of night,

Paint stars as fast and as many as you can.

Hold fast to the canvas and crawl in;

A festoon of night; a festival of stars.

Pretend you are born of stars.

Do not hear the chime of little clocks that announce the hour.

Hurl your body to Orion.

Now the stars are thick and fast.

They blaze in a portrait of sheer light.

The little clocks of gold are stopped in time.

Encompass each band of blinding light.

Your hour has come.

Voices from outside night's portrait call to you,

But your canvas is already painted.

In night there is vision.

Leap upon the star-time;

The big time revelry.

Summer

The roses bathed in summer take my breath away.

The dragonflies dancing with orange monarch butterflies,

Give me a taste of joy.

The caw-caw of the black crows deliver life.

In summer I touch heat and lazily walk

Through the periwinkle morning glories

And the white spilling Queen Ann's lace.

I lay me down in clover green

And study the branches of bark of the high trees.

A breeze fans the green veined leaves

And the white puff of cloud drifts in the sky.

A child picks a buttercup and puts its yellow fullness under my chin,

To see if I like butter.

She says you do, you do.

Butter in summer.

The Beautiful Ones

All the beautiful ones come to me; all the beautiful ones pray for me.

They come from on high. Their wings beat all around me.

They do not abandon me. They never leave me alone.

Their eyes are soft and true.

Their nature deeply caring and profound.

I see the beautiful ones and they see me.

All my being is raised high and free. All my desire comes to pass.

The beautiful ones are by my side.

They bless my soul with life and unending fire.

When I open my eyes sometimes for the first time;

I witness the new sight I am given.

I raise my eyes to be with my beautiful ones.

The Bride

I am a night bride.

My gown casts a glow in the dark.

I am a night bride.

The groom is a shadow.

Tenderly I hold night orchids in my arms.

The splendor of the occasion is all around me.

I invite the moon and stars to be my guests for the night bride.

I walk barefoot down the bridal path.

The shadow of my groom is beside me.

The train of my gown swishes in the uncut grasses.

I stop in a meadow. Who calls my name?

It is the shadow of the groom.

Who gives me away? The moon and stars do.

My orchids are intoxicating to me; the bride.

The China Distance

Weep not for me. Angels have lingered within my tears.

Hold not a vigil. I have lit candles to encircle the moon.

A dress sewn with delicate thread is mine.

Woven of silk, perhaps it belongs to China.

I have traveled continents on bare feet;

Sprigs of red berries in my black hair.

There you stand unsure what language I speak.

All the while you do understand.

Travel not over seas for me. I can make my way.

Only leave a door open for me.

You will hear my brass keys jingle.

Perhaps they joined within locks of doors: the continent of China.

I have lit candles to show me the way.

Here, there it is only a question of distances crossed.

I was born with the moon encircling me.

The angels have lingered a lifetime for me.

I believe you once glimpsed me in China.

The silk is real enough.

The Dusk Hour

It is the dusk hour; summer dusk time.

The fading orange and pink sky casts a calm on earth.

Summer flowers fragrance the air.

Their green leaves and vibrant colors wave in the breeze:

indigo, red like cherries, and yellow as deep as the sun.

The landscape settles into itself.

It is the dusk hour: the time of days' reflection.

The leaves of trees rustle in the breeze.

The lace curtains within open windows gently wave.

Ripe watermelon and ice cream have their place with laughing children.

Playful dogs circle and bark excitedly.

The languid hour of life is pulsing with pleasure upon the horizon.

The Embrace

I give you all my blessings in a circle of light.
I give you all my joys in a circle of peace.
You will shine; oh yes, you will shine before me.
My eyes will catch a glimmer of your soul.
Your soul speaks to me as does rain to heaven.
Embrace.
Embrace.
Embrace me.
I feel your joy like a thousand stars.
I know your heart, for I know your soul; pure and whole.
I gather you close to my breast that I might hold you in your entirety.
Your soul speaks to me as does rain to heaven.
Embrace.
Embrace.
Embrace me.

The Extension

Within the cusp of your Sonata there are no abbreviations.

Your rhythm is steady with intent.

There is a symphony because you make it so.

Poised with instruments you play. The music is personal.

Plucking strings and sustaining the woodwinds you keep time.

Breathe. Sustain. Breathe. Sustain.

The timing is personal.

There are no abbreviations where intent is concerned.

I take a good look; long and steady.

My movements sustain me.

Breathe. Sustain. Breathe. Sustain.

I will keep time and position all the necessary parts

To respond at a moment's glance. I understand the pulse.

Sustain. Comprehend. Sustain. Comprehend. Breathe.

The Eyes That Dazzle

Your eyes dazzle my heart.

Your arms are jewels that wrap around me.

Your hair is a river that flows through my hands.

Your voice is a harp that brings music to my ears.

The day rises with your presence;

As does the night rest with it.

You are the angel of my soul.

When you weep, the heavens shed tears with you.

When you laugh, the sun's rays shine upon you.

When you pray, God's blessings hold you and keep you.

When you sing, the birds of the forest follow suit by the multitudes.

Where you walk, I follow completely.

The First and the Last

The first word I utter is silent.

The first step I take leaves no impression in the sand.

The first leaf that falls is lost to the winds.

The first tear I shed is dry.

The first dress I wear is without color.

The first time I love is without ecstasy.

The first flame I burn is without fire.

The last word I utter is heard.

The last step I take creates an impression in the sand.

The last leaf that falls is found by the winds.

The last tear I cry is wet.

The last dress I wear is adorned with color.

The last time I love is with passion.

The last flame I burn ignites a multitude of sparks.

The Frost Time

Breath upon my breath.

Sway I to a waltz in the forest.

The frost does not reach me.

Tall and mighty partners are the trees.

I dance.

My thighs are free.

The range of song of the fall birds carry high to the heavens.

No thorns touch my heart.

Locked away are the pungent smells of this season time.

A late acorn drops down to the pine needles.

I want a place here to cherish small things.

Lands my heart with the hard acorns.

Anoints me with heat.

In the late colorless grasses I gather momentum and I reap.

The Gathering

Can you speak of the great gathering?

All the people of the earth shall be as one.

Will you attend and partake of your portion?

Every soul will be of one mind.

Every beating of every heart will exemplify a bonding of spirits.

Gather, yes gather and be as one.

Speak neither of division nor of inconsequential differences.

All differences shall be laid to rest.

Gather to share this long awaited day.

There shall be neither scorn nor jealousy.

All will be one.

There is a calling to rejoice within the land.

Come at last to this great gathering.

The Great Secret

Peering from behind rocks I see you.

I want to touch you but I am rocks away.

Your name is my flame. You mold with the waves.

Diving I murmur your name. A great secret eclipses the time.

I behold your essence. Your face is a mystery of mine.

Pressing rock I inscribe the flame. Your face lives in my eyes.

Dare I cross the great divide for fear of a name?

Clandestine heart of mine.

Your face, shiny with brine, kisses the ocean.

My palms are craggy rocks away.

I press my face to your name. Telepathy will save me.

Love makes my bones quiver.

Secrets make you accessible to step across time.

From a great distance I embrace you.

All this time you sensed my presence.

I did not dare to know.

You call my name.

The great secret will never be the same.

The Journey

Blow the wind.

Sail the ship.

Far. Far out.

Beyond the horizon.

I hail from the port to the bow.

The stern is my compass.

There is the murmur of evening.

The sails are mighty.

Entice the current.

Heaving the wood into a rhythm upon the sea.

Open. Full sail ahead.

Call to the underbelly of approaching stars.

I steer onward port to bow.

My masts do wave to the Northern star.

Beckons the harbor but I am bound for parts unknown.

The great ocean leaps with majesty born to infinite destinations.

Lie low the last wisp of light.

Driven am I to the port, the bow, the mast and the night.

The Magic Girl

The magic girl floats by and in her palms she caresses a white dove.

The magic girl floats by and a melody is all around her.

The magic girl floats by dressed all in pink, she floats surrounded by beauty.

The magic girl spins a pinwheel within the wisps of cloud.

The magic girl carries a bundle of hearts, she scatters them upon earth.

Singing, she is singing of love.

The magic girl floats by and dances upon ocean waves,

The pink of her dress dances too.

The magic girl floats by and in her palms she caresses a white dove.

The Northern Star

The last light of day is falling.

The Northern Star appears.

The children are gathered.

Mothers prepare the evening meal.

Soft shadows surround a multitude of houses.

The warmth of day lingers yet.

Voices emanate around the dinner table.

Lamps cast soft light in the corners of each room.

Night descends full of stars.

Children's laughter is heard in the soothing waters of the cleansing baths.

Toys of every kind float on the surface.

Bubbles of soap appear like miniature rainbows, iridescent and round.

A lullaby is heard from the baby's room.

Her voice rises and falls from deep within her breast.

She gently leaves.

Her scent remains in the air.

The baby sleeps with long steady breaths.

The Northern Star glows.

The Straddling Time

He falls out of the ochre skies like a flame upon me.

He whispers I am the one.

A cloud of vermilion is unleashed.

Unlacing his boots he breaks into song.

I am the one he echoes, braving the hills.

Hitching the sky and night together he rides.

Straddling a blazing hunger,

His loins are thrown into a rythem pulsing time.

I am the one.

He conquers all that night has to offer.

I am the one, he sings, as he flies.

For Harold Bond

The Union

Slowly you ascend the plateau.

The wind is high above you. The gods speak.

Expands the universe. The plateau too.

Above is the wind. A voice. A revelation of height.

Far below rock penetrates time. Blue sky rests firmly.

Plummets the great time-drop of destiny. Stone to sky.

The gods prophesize for you the eye of sheer formation.

The density of sky and rock and cloud increases.

Above you give voice to a voice.

The gods portend their vision and you listen.

Imbibe them:

Until the limitless exaltations of all that came to be here is yours.

You hold fast: to sky and stone,

And undertones of a vastness that pervades.

Intone breath with the gods beside you.

The Wand

The wand is waved. It is the good witch.

Silver Star dust floats. The superb voices alight.

They whisper, take the bounty. Silver encircles the palm.

Chant the song of angels. Immerse this moment upon the soul.

The goodness in the heart of night surrounds the spirit in entirety.

Nuances of breath and time are released.

Slowly the night circles; a convocation.

The wand is waved. The granting is good.

The night spirits speak. Take.

Embrace the harmony of the elements; earth, air, fire and water.

The empathy of destinies accompanies every step along the journey.

Nocturnal dreams stir amid the star-lit branches.

The laying on of unseen hands heals the senses.

Silver encircles the palm.

Fathom every touch upon the flesh.

It is good.

Treasures

My belly is a sieve.

I retain rubies, emeralds and diamonds.

My jewels are rich and deep. My wealth is a river flowing.

I drink from the five rivers of a vast ocean.

Starfish and conch shells,

Sea glass and glistening scales of fish surround me.

Adorn me.

The water of life sustains me.

I string pearls from oyster shells and call them my own.

I am the ebb and flow of tide.

I recline high in the cave cliffs and rest upon sea sponges.

Weave upon my body mire and incense.

Treasure footprints of mine in the sand.

Imprint my navel upon your forehead,

To remember the day the sieve did open.

Water Lily Kisses

Lilies of the water drift to my eyes.

The silken petals are languid as they sway upon water.

Love of the lover is inspired to rise.

I portend the kiss upon their lips.

Water lilies envelop as they ease into water.

The kiss I thought so far away is now upon my lips.

Reflections of every kiss transcend water and lilies.

Imagine the moment.

It will come.

The water lilies are languid in our eyes.

Their petals fan out and hold each second:

Rare and unspoken,

Inspired and desired,

While the lovers' kiss ripples and

Caresses the day beautifully; serenely within this hour.

When You Tell Them

When you tell them about me:

Tell them I saved my hours in a little paper cup for you.

When you tell them about me:

Tell them I wore red velvet dresses for you.

When you tell them about me:

Tell them how I bowed my head in gratitude for you.

When you tell them about me:

Tell them how I collected little trinkets of gold for you.

When you rise up and drink your morning coffee:

See me in the swirling liquid you bring to your lips.

When you tell them about me:

Tell them how I loved you.

Wine

Drink of the wine.

It will sustain you.

Libation that only the gods know.

Drink of the wine, as it opens locked doors to the heart and soul.

The wine touches your lips and pulses warmth through your being.

Empty your glass as you reach for your lover.

Drink of the wine.

Spill not a drop.

Offer it up to the gods in a moment of praise for pleasure.

Indulge in kisses with your lover for he is the key to

The sharing of wine on a moonlit evening.

This is the moment.

The pouring; then the tasting of wine-touched lips.

Your Faith

Wrap your faith thickly around you

To stave off cruelty and the demise of your world.

Wrap your faith around your heart

For the heart is vulnerable and open.

Hide your eyes from darkness

That you may see clearly and far before you.

Sing with a closed mouth.

You know your song.

Wrap your faith tightly around your body

That nobody may strike you down as you walk.

Pay close attention to your hands

For they express what is in your soul.

Let your faith be your bed

For that is where you rest within.

Then sing with open mouth.

Your faith is safe.

Your Name

Holy is your name.

I believe with every flower unfurling its petals

That you exist.

Every hand I hold; every bit of love is holy.

See me pray among my own scriptures for everyday is a blessing.

Every human being that I hold dear is blessed and holy unto me.

Divine and holy is the light that emanates from your eyes.

Each convocation strengthens our unity.

Do not weep for you are never alone.

The stream of untapped waters is before you;

Beside you; within you.

Come let us embrace each blessing.

978-0-595-42210-4
0-595-42210-1

Printed in the United States
81030LV00005B/631-648